1979

The Variorum
Civil Disobedience

Also by Walter Harding

The Variorum Walden

The Variorum
Civil
Disobedience

by HENRY DAVID THOREAU

*Annotated and with
an Introduction by*
WALTER HARDING

Twayne Publishers, Inc   ::   New York

CONTENTS

PART I

A Brief History

INTRODUCTION

I

One evening late in July of 1846, probably the 23rd or 24th, Thoreau walked in to Concord village from Walden Pond to pick up a shoe he had left at the cobbler's shop to be repaired. He was stopped on the street by Sam Staples, the local constable, tax collector, and jailer, and asked to pay his poll tax for the last several years. "I'll pay your tax, Henry, if you're hard up," Staples said. He also offered to try to persuade the selectmen to reduce the tax if Thoreau thought it too high, but Thoreau replied that he had not paid it as a matter of principle and didn't intend to pay it now. When Staples asked what he should do about it, Thoreau suggested that if he didn't like it, he could resign his office. But Staples, not taking kindly to that suggestion, replied, "Henry, if you don't pay, I shall have to lock you up pretty soon." "As well now as any time, Sam," was the answer. "Well, come along then," said Staples, and took him to jail.

Thoreau was not the first to be arrested in Concord for non-payment of his poll taxes. More than three years before, on January 17, 1843, Staples had arrested Thoreau's friend, Bronson Alcott, on the same charge. The Massachusetts poll tax (not a voting tax, but a head tax imposed on every male between the ages of twenty and seventy) had long been unpopular, and the Abolitionists seized upon protesting against paying it as a dra-

11

matic way of demonstrating their abhorrence of a government that supported slavery. Although Alcott was arrested, he was never jailed, for Squire Hoar, the town's leading citizen, paid Alcott's taxes himself rather than permit such a blot on the town escutcheon. And in the succeeding years, despite his pleas for "the privilege of non-payment of taxes," Alcott's wife's family paid his taxes in advance to avoid the embarrassment of having a relative in jail. In December 1843 Alcott's English friend, Charles Lane, also refused to pay his poll tax in Concord and was arrested. Again Squire Hoar paid the tax, and Lane was quickly released.

The examples of Alcott and Lane set Thoreau to thinking. The agitation against slavery had grown in recent years from the work of a few rare individuals to that of the beginnings of a mass movement. William Lloyd Garrison was beginning to become a household name. Ex-President John Quincy Adams, through his constant barrage of petitions and speeches in the national House of Representatives, was slowly making more and more people aware of the vast gap between the democratic principles the country vocally avowed and the slavery legally practiced in the South. The antislavery movement had by no means attained respectability (ironically it was not to attain that until after the Civil War when the need for its activities no longer existed), and Garrison could still be dragged through the streets of Boston with a noose around his neck. But at least it was causing twinges in the American conscience.

Thoreau himself was made particularly aware of the issues involved by the antislavery activities of the members of his own household—his mother and sisters—by the antislavery periodicals they regularly subscribed to, and by the fact that the antislavery agitators who visited Concord invariably put up for the night in his mother's boarding house. It is safe to say that there was probably hardly a single prominent New England abolitionist of those times that Thoreau did not meet at least once across his mother's dining table.

12

The abolitionists had, in recent years, split, philosophically at least, into two groups. Those led by William Lloyd Garrison were activists. They denounced loudly and vehemently those institutions such as the church, the state, and the press which they felt were the most ardent defenders of the status quo on the slavery question. Feeling their only weapon against these institutions to be mass action, they stressed the development of larger and more aggressive antislavery societies. The other group, which until his recent death had been led by Nathaniel P. Rogers, believed the only possible solution was the reformation of mankind. They feared that Garrison's plans would lead to the institutionalizing of the antislavery societies themselves and argued that a utopian society could be achieved only through self-reformation of each individual in a society. This kind of a philosophy was inevitably attractive to a Transcendentalist such as Thoreau. He had already endorsed Rogers' principles in the pages of *The Dial*. Now that he felt called to action himself, he quite naturally took the individualistic rather than the organizational approach, and adopting the ideas and actions of Lane and Alcott, he refused to pay his own poll tax.

Unfortunately for Thoreau's principles, Staples for several years simply ignored Thoreau's tax resistance. Although Staples, like many of the "more practical" townspeople, was pretty skeptical of the "Transcendentalist crowd" (he used to say of Emerson, "I suppose there's a great many things that Mr. Emerson knows that I couldn't understand; but I *know* that there's a damn sight of things that I know that he don't know anything about"), he always had a high opinion of Thoreau. Therefore, if Thoreau chose to ignore paying his taxes, Staples chose to ignore his non-payment.

Why Staples suddenly decided to take action in the summer of 1846 is not known for certain. He was about to give up his position as tax collector and so might have been faced with the prospect of paying Thoreau's taxes himself to clear the books. Or it might have been that the recent declaration of war against

Mexico had inflamed a patriotism that demanded the collection of all taxes. At any rate, he gave Thoreau several warnings before finally arresting him and said afterwards that he was not worried about Thoreau's running off; he knew he could get him when he wanted to.

The Concord jail, now long since torn down, was no small-town lockup. Concord was the shire town of Middlesex County and this was the county jail. It stood just off the Mill Dam, behind the stores, near the present site of the Roman Catholic rectory, and was built of granite, three stories high, sixty-five feet long, thirty-two feet wide, and surrounded with a brick wall about ten feet high, mounted with iron pickets. It had eighteen cells, each twenty-six feet long and eight and a half feet high. Each cell had two double-grated windows. A formidable jail indeed.

The prisoners were enjoying a chat and the evening air in the prison yard when Thoreau and Staples entered. Staples told the men it was time to return to their cells and introduced Thoreau to his cellmate. When the door was locked, he showed Thoreau where to hang his hat and how to manage matters there. After inquiring about Thoreau's arrest, he explained that he had been accused of burning down a barn and had been waiting three months for his trial—although since he was given free board and room and was permitted to go out and work in the hayfields by the day, he thought he was being well treated and was contented.

Thoreau made the most of what he thought to be a rare opportunity and pumped his cellmate for all he was worth about the history of the jail and its occupants and its gossip, which he realized never circulated outside, but eventually his informant tired of the inquisition and went to bed, leaving Thoreau to blow out the lamp. Thoreau, however, was much too excited to sleep and stood at the window for some time, looking out through the grating and listening to the activities in the nearby hotel. Later in the night a prisoner in a nearby cell began calling out with painful monotony, "What is life? So this is life!" Finally tiring of the repetition, Thoreau put his head to the window bars and called out in a loud voice, "Well, what *is* life, then?" His only answer was silence and his reward a quiet night's sleep.

Meanwhile, word of Thoreau's arrest had rapidly spread through the village. When his mother heard of it, she rushed to the jail to ascertain the truth of the rumor and then back home to tell the family the news. Sam Staples had gone out for a while that evening, and on his return his daughter Ellen informed him that someone had knocked at the door in his absence and, passing in a package, had said, "Here is the money to pay Mr. Thoreau's tax." Staples had taken off his boots and was sitting by the fire when his daughter told him, and he declared that he wasn't going to take the trouble to put them back on. Thoreau could just as well spend the night in jail and be released in the morning.

Just who the person was who knocked on Staples' door and handed in the package has never been absolutely ascertained. Some have claimed that it was Emerson; others, Aunt Jane Thoreau, Elizabeth Hoar, Rockwood Hoar, or Samuel Hoar. Staples, himself, told so many stories in later years—that it was a man, a young woman, an old woman, two women—that his word, as he readily admitted to one of his inquisitors, was not to be depended on. As a matter of fact, neither he nor his daughter probably ever knew, for tradition has it that the person was heavily veiled. But the preponderance of evidence points to Aunt Maria Thoreau. And Eben J. Loomis, who was an old friend of the Thoreau family, was almost certain in his old age that Aunt Maria had once admitted to him that she was the one.

Probably what happened is that when Thoreau's mother returned home with the news, Aunt Maria was understandably upset to learn that her nephew was in jail. It seems likely that Thoreau had extracted a promise from his mother not to interfere with his plans. But Aunt Maria was bound by no such promise and so stepped in and paid the tax. And regularly thereafter,

15

possibly even until the time of Thoreau's death, she or others paid his tax in advance so that the incident could not occur again.

When morning came, the prisoners were fed their breakfast of bread and a pint of chocolate, and Thoreau's cellmate, leaving for his day's stint in the hayfields, bade him goodbye, saying that he doubted if he would see Thoreau again. (Later Thoreau was to find out that when his cellmate came to trial, he was found innocent of the charges and released. Apparently he had fallen asleep in the barn while smoking and so had inadvertently burned it down.)

When Staples came to release Thoreau, he was astounded to discover that Thoreau was not willing to leave the jail, the only prisoner he ever had who did not want to leave as soon as he could. In fact, said Staples, Thoreau was "as mad as the devil" at being released. It had been the whole purpose of his refusal to pay taxes to get arrested and so to call dramatically to the attention of his fellow citizens the cause of abolitionism that he had espoused. When Aunt Maria paid his taxes, she had destroyed the whole point of his campaign, and, to put it mildly, he was not pleased. Since he himself had not paid those taxes, he felt he had the right to stay in jail and said so. But Staples said, "Henry, if you will not go of your own accord I shall put you out, for you cannot stay here any longer." Capitulating, Thoreau finally went on his way, picked up his shoe at the cobbler's, and within a half an hour was picking huckleberries on a hill two miles off where, as he said rejoicingly, "the State was nowhere to be seen."

Word of his arrest and release had, of course, spread rapidly throughout the town. Many stared at him, he noticed, as though he had been on a long journey. And little Georgie Bartlett said that he thought from the excitement he was seeing a Siberian exile or John Bunyan himself. Many of his townsmen of course did not agree with or approve of Thoreau's action. James Garty, who readily admitted that Thoreau "was a good

16

sort of man " and "would pay every cent he owed to any man," complained at the time that "it wouldn't do to have everybody like him, or his way of thinking." Emerson complained to Bronson Alcott that Thoreau's action was "mean and skulking, and in bad taste"; but Alcott, in reply, defended it as a good example of "dignified noncompliance with the injunction of civil powers." Emerson then sputtered in his journal: "The State is a poor, good beast who means the best: it means friendly. A poor cow who does well by you,—do not grudge it its hay. . . . As long as the state means you well, do not refuse your pistareen. You have a tottering cause: ninety parts of the pistareen it will spend for what you think also good: ten parts for mischief. . . . In the particular, it is worth considering that refusing payment of the state tax does not reach the evil so nearly as many other methods within your reach. . . . The prison is one step to suicide." And when Emerson next met Thoreau, he asked him why he had gone to jail, only to have Thoreau aptly reply, "Why did you not?" Emerson, on further thought, finally admitted in his journal that Thoreau's position was at least stronger than the Abolitionists who denounce the war and yet pay the tax.

As for Sam Staples, his relations with Thoreau continued as amiable as ever. There is a legend that Alcott once, when pestered by Staples for his taxes, picked all the potato bugs off his own vines and dumped them into Staples' garden in retaliation. But Thoreau carried no such grudge. In later years he often hired Staples as his assistant when he was surveying. And Staples, in his turn, often boasted that Thoreau was his most distinguished prisoner.

So many of Thoreau's townsmen expressed a curiosity about his actions and wanted to know the rationale for his trying to go to jail that Thoreau finally wrote out an explanation and delivered it as a lecture on "the relation of the individual to the State" at the Concord Lyceum on January 26, 1848. He found an attentive audience, and Bronson Alcott, at least, "took great

17

pleasure" in the lecture. Three weeks later, by request, he gave the same lecture again so others of his townsmen could hear.

In the spring of 1849 Elizabeth Peabody suddenly wrote to ask Thoreau for permission to publish that lecture. She was establishing a new periodical to be called *Aesthetic Papers* to carry along the Transcendentalist message where *The Dial* had dropped it, and wanted to include his lecture in the first (and what later turned out to be the only) issue. Thoreau at the moment was busy correcting proofs of his first book and replied that he hardly had time left for bodily exercise, let alone copying out an old lecture. Nonetheless he promised to send the manuscript along within a week, but he cautioned her that it was offered for use in her first volume only. He had had enough of delaying actions on the part of editors.

Miss Peabody, however, kept her word. Six weeks later, on May 14, 1849, she published her magazine containing pieces by Emerson and Hawthorne along with Thoreau's essay, now entitled "Resistance to Civil Government." (It did not receive its more widely known title of "Civil Disobedience" until it was collected into his *Yankee in Canada, with Anti-Slavery and Reform Papers* in 1866, four years after his death.)

At the time of its publication, however, the essay produced scarcely a ripple. Although *Aesthetic Papers* was noticed here and there, the reviewers generally ignored Thoreau's contribution. They were more interested in the essays by the better-known Emerson and Hawthorne in the same issue. The one exception was a review by Sophia Dobson Collet in the *People's Review* in London, England. She quoted several of the meatiest paragraphs and prefaced them with the comment that "as it is not likely to be much known in England, we give the following extracts, premising that it ought to be read as a whole to be thoroughly appreciated." But except for Miss Collet's comment, the essay was ignored.

II

The central points of Thoreau's essay are these:

(1) There is a "higher law" than the law of one's land. That is the law of the conscience, the "inner voice," the "oversoul"—call it what you will.

(2) On those rare occasions when this "higher law" and the law of the land come in conflict, it is one's duty to obey that "higher law" and deliberately violate the law of the land.

(3) If one deliberately violates the law of the land, he must be willing to take the full consequences of that action, even to the point of going to jail.

(4) However, going to jail is not necessarily the negative act it might seem, for it will serve to draw the attention of men of good will to the evil law and thus help to bring about its repeal. Or, if enough men go to jail, their acts will serve to clog the machinery of the state and thus make the evil law unenforceable.

These theories are not original with Thoreau. Socrates in drinking the cup of hemlock and Antigone in sprinkling dust on the body of Polyneices were both committing acts of civil disobedience. Boethius many centuries ago expounded the philosophy in western culture and Mencius in eastern. But the important fact is that it was Thoreau who popularized the idea, though it was half a century after the essay appeared in print before anyone paid any serious attention to it.

About 1900 the Russian novelist and philosopher Count Leo Tolstoy somewhere, somehow, ran across the essay and was struck with its implications concerning his own attempts to better the conditions of the Russian serfs under Czarist domination. But so far as I have been able to find out, the only direct action he ever took with Thoreau's ideas was to write a letter to the *North*

American Review asking the American people why they did not pay more attention to the voice of Thoreau than to that of their financial and industrial millionaires and their successful generals and admirals.

True credit for the rediscovery of Thoreau's "Civil Disobedience" should go to a young Hindu law student by the name of Mohandas K. Gandhi who was studying at Oxford University in England about 1900. Gandhi, because of his religion, was a vegetarian. Having difficulty finding food proper to his diet on the university campus, he quite naturally got in touch with some of the English vegetarians—one Henry Stephens Salt in particular. Salt was, by chance, the author of an excellent biography of Thoreau and the editor of several collections of Thoreau's works. Gandhi caught some of Salt's enthusiasm for Thoreau and began to read whatever of his works he could lay hold of. After his graduation from Oxford, Gandhi established himself as a lawyer in South Africa, devoting himself primarily to the defense of violators of the discriminatory laws passed against the members of his own race. To unite the Indian residents of South Africa he established a newspaper entitled *Indian Opinion*. And therein, in the issue of October 26, 1907, he printed Thoreau's "Civil Disobedience," later reprinting it in pamphlet form for wider distribution. He accompanied the essay with editorials advocating the use of civil disobedience against the offensive legislation. He offered prizes for student essays on the most effective methods of passive resistance. And he led direct action against the laws, deliberately violating them to bring about mass arrest. Progress was at first slow, but the movement gradually gained momentum, and eventually the government was forced to choose between enforcing the laws and glutting the jails with hundreds and even thousands of violators. The laws were one by one repealed or became dead letters. Civil disobedience had triumphed.

Word of the effectiveness of Gandhi's Thoreauvian methods soon spread to his native land, where a movement to free the country from British domination was getting under way. Gandhi, at the strong request of his native countrymen, returned to India to lead the movement. For thirty years he conducted civil disobedience campaigns the length and breadth of the country. When the British government, wishing to establish a lucrative monopoly, forbade the manufacture of salt, Gandhi led followers to the seashore, there to symbolically violate the law by producing salt through sea-water evaporation a cupful at a time. As he fully expected, he was immediately arrested and jailed. But the government found it had not solved its problem. In the eyes of his countrymen Gandhi had become a martyr to their own cause, and they rushed forward by the hundreds and thousands to join his movement and to duplicate his violation of the law. In prison Gandhi went on a hunger strike protesting what he considered his illegal arrest. As he sank lower and lower, more and more sympathy was aroused for him, not only in India but around the world. Rather than risk having him die on their hands, the government freed him. As soon as he was physically able, he violated the salt law once again and was once again put into prison. It was a cat-and-mouse game, but eventually public opinion forced the government to abandon the law. Gandhi then turned his attention to other unjust laws. The action and the reaction were repeated again and again. To make a long story short, India under Gandhi's leadership and using Thoreau's techniques of civil disobedience eventually won complete freedom in 1945.

Gandhi directed his techniques not only against unjust governmental laws but also against equally unjust religious codes. The social structure of Hinduism was based upon a caste system. The lowest group, but the largest numerically, was the so-called Untouchables. Over and over again they found the religious codes turned against them. Let us take a single striking example. The only source of water for many Indian villages was a single well. Since the upper-caste Hindus used the well, the lower-caste Untouchables were forbidden to go near it. They were forced to resort to the open streams and pools. Because of the vast overpopulation of India, all of these sources of water were badly polluted. The Untouchables quite understandably died off like the proverbial flies. When Gandhi found that pleas as to the inhumanity of the religious codes went unheeded, he led the Untouchables to the wells and joined them in filling jars of water. Civil police were called in to enforce the religious laws, and the violators were at first attacked unmercifully. When local police, sickened by the violence used on the passive resisters, refused to enforce the laws, special military police recruited from a notoriously bloodthirsty tribe on the Himalayan border were brought in. But they too eventually found their sympathies won by the martyrdom of the Untouchables and refused to continue their violence. The laws became unenforceable and the Untouchables won their right to use the village wells. Once again Gandhi's Thoreauvian civil disobedience had won.

Some years ago Roger Baldwin, then the director of the American Civil Liberties Union, told me that he once took a long train journey with Gandhi. When Gandhi learned that Mr. Baldwin had been born and brought up in Massachusetts near Thoreau's Concord, he plied him with questions about Thoreau's life and showed him that he was carrying a copy of "Civil Disobedience" in his luggage. He said he never went anywhere—not even to jail—without a copy of the pamphlet because it epitomized the whole spirit of his life.

But we need not confine ourselves to India. "Civil Disobedience" has had a world-wide influence. Let us turn to Denmark for another example. Henry David Thoreau is virtually a folk-hero in Denmark today. Why? Because "Civil Disobedience" was used as a manual of arms by the resistance movement against the Nazi invasion during World War II. It was circulated surreptitiously throughout the war years among the Danes as a means of encouraging them to further acts of resistance. What was the result? Well, let me give a few examples. When the Nazis invoked a law requiring all Jews to wear a large six-pointed yellow star on the back of each article of clothing—the

22

obvious purpose being to single out the Jews for further persecution—virtually every citizen in Denmark, Jew or Gentile, including even King Christian, appeared in the streets wearing the yellow star. The law was thus nullified.

When the King took part in numerous such actions, the Nazis felt obliged to retaliate. But they did not dare to execute or even to arrest the King. They took what they thought was the easiest way out by confining the King to his palace and announcing simply that he was ill. But the Danish people quickly caught on, and citizens from all over the country decided to "say it with flowers." Going to their local florists, they ordered bouquets to be sent to the King—what could seemingly be more harmless? But what was the result? Every road leading into Copenhagen, the capital city, and every street within the city was soon blocked with florists delivering flowers to the King. Traffic could not move. Business could not be conducted. The entire city came to a standstill. Yet people obviously could not be punished for sending flowers. The Nazis were forced to announce that the King had suddenly miraculously recovered and to give him complete freedom of his country for the rest of the years of the invasion. These are only two of many examples of the influence of Thoreau's "Civil Disobedience" in Denmark, but they give some idea of why the Nazis thought the Danes to be the most recalcitrant of all their subjects during the war.

But now let us return to the United States. Has "Civil Disobedience" had any influence here? First you may be surprised to learn of the amount of official resistance there has been to the essay in this our democratic country. Upton Sinclair, the novelist; Norman Thomas, the perennial candidate of the Socialist Party; and Emma Goldman, the anarchist editor of *Mother Earth*, have each been arrested for reading Thoreau's essay from the public platform—Sinclair during a labor strike in California in the early 1930's; Thomas during a protest against the machine rule of Frank ("I am the law") Hague of Jersey City in the late 1930's; and Emma Goldman during protest rallies

23

against the conscription act of 1917. Or again, in the 1930's, the entire edition of one issue of *Heresia,* an Italian-language newspaper in New York City, was confiscated and destroyed by the New York City police because it included a translation of "Civil Disobedience"—this despite the fact that at that very time anyone could go into any bookstore in New York City and purchase an edition of "Civil Disobedience" in English without the least difficulty. To cite still another example of official resistance, when, in the mid-1950's, the United States Information Service included as a standard book in all their libraries around the world a textbook of American literature which reprinted Thoreau's "Civil Disobedience," the late Senator Joseph McCarthy of Wisconsin succeeded in having that book removed from the shelves of each of those libraries—specifically because of the Thoreau essay.

But despite the occasional official opposition—and I in all fairness must stress that the opposition has only been very, very occasional—"Civil Disobedience" has had a continuing influence in this country. I have never been able to discover a direct connection between Thoreau's essay and the famous sit-down strikes led by the C.I.O. during the depression years, but certainly it would be difficult to discover any more practical application of the ideas that Thoreau advocated than those were.

For many years the pacifist movement in this country (and incidentally in England, France, and South America, too), although very small and comparatively uninfluential, has stimulated the publication and distribution of Thoreau's essay. I have in my files numerous editions of "Civil Disobedience" printed by such groups. Many of the conscientious objectors who were imprisoned during World War II quoted Thoreau's essay in defense of their actions. And I know of at least one who took a copy of "Civil Disobedience" to prison with him.

I understand that there is a small group of pacifists who even now each year file a copy of "Civil Disobedience" in lieu of an income tax report, implying by the action that they refuse to underwrite our military budget. I might add that I understand in such cases the Federal Income Tax Bureau, acting as did Thoreau's Aunt Maria, steps in and pays the tax—but with the significant difference that the Income Tax Bureau then confiscates that sum out of the individual's bank account or salary. But the objectors feel that at least the protest has been made. A few years ago when a number of pacifists were protesting the construction of nuclear submarines at New London, Connecticut, they conducted their protest in a rowboat named "Henry D. Thoreau."

A more striking example of Thoreau's influence in our country today however is that of the antisegregation movement throughout the South. The refusal of Negroes to ride segregated buses in Montgomery, Alabama; the boycotting by Negroes of segregated stores in Albany, Georgia; the kneel-ins of Negroes in the white churches of Nashville, Tennessee; the "Freedom" riders in Alabama and Mississippi—each and every one of these is a very specific example of the influence of Thoreau. And let me cite as proof of that, the words of two of the outstanding leaders of the movement. First, the Rev. James Robinson, former pastor of the Church of the Master in Harlem, now director of "Operation Crossroads" (the International Voluntary Work Camps) for the United States in Africa, and one of the most influential Negroes in this country, said in an article on "Civil Disobedience" twenty years ago, that was addressed to the group who later founded CORE (the Committee on Racial Equality):

Thoreau's Civil Disobedience was not used much by the Abolitionists for whom it was written; probably no one before Gandhi realized its significance for a new type of social movement based upon group discipline and personal conscience. As one reads this essay, it is impossible not to notice that almost every sentence is loaded with meaning for us today. . . . Substitute the economic, political, and social persecution of American Negroes today where Thoreau condemns Negro slavery—and you will scarcely find half a dozen sentences in the entire essay which you cannot apply to your own actions in the present crisis.

I have no doubt but his article led in part at least to the establishment of CORE.

And second, Rev. Martin Luther King, who is universally recognized as the leader of the current struggles for human rights in the South today, tells us in his autobiography, *Stride Toward Freedom*:

When I went to Atlanta's Morehouse College as a freshman in 1944 my concern for racial and economic justice was already substantial. During my student days at Morehouse I read Thoreau's "Essay on Civil Disobedience" for the first time. Fascinated by the idea of refusing to cooperate with an evil system, I was so deeply moved that I reread the work several times. This was my first intellectual contact with the theory of nonviolent resistance.

And then, speaking of the boycott he organized against segregated buses in Montgomery, Alabama, he says:

At this point I began to think about Thoreau's "Essay on Civil Disobedience." I remembered how, as a college student, I had been moved when I first read this work. I became convinced that what we were preparing to do in Montgomery was related to what Thoreau had expressed. We were simply saying to the white community, "We can no longer lend our cooperation to an evil system."

Something began to say to me, "He who passively accepts evil is as much involved in it as he who helps to perpetuate it. He who accepts evil without protesting against it is really cooperating with it." When oppressed people willingly accept their oppression they only serve to give the oppressor a convenient justification for his acts. Often the oppressor goes along unaware of the evil involved in his oppression so long as the oppressed accepts it. So in order to be true to one's conscience and true to God, a righteous man has no alternative but to refuse to cooperate with an evil system. This

26

I felt was the nature of our action. From this moment on I conceived of our movement as an act of massive non-cooperation.

Unquestionably, then, Thoreau's century-old essay has had and is having a powerful influence on the fight for Negro rights in our country today . . . an influence as profound as it had in South Africa fifty years ago or India of thirty years ago or Denmark of twenty years ago. Its influence has traveled around the world and now has returned home.

No stronger evidence is needed that the civil disobedience that Thoreau advocated has become a part of the American way of life than the opposition to the war in Vietnam. The widespread appearance of protesters from the college campus to the New York Stock Exchange, along the major avenues of cities and at major industrial and military sites, at the White House and the Pentagon—as well as the public burning of draft cards by young men—all attest to the fact that, though it took a century, the American people have become aware of the usefulness and validity of Thoreau's theory.

A NOTE ON THE TEXT

Thoreau's "Civil Disobedience" exists in two slightly differing versions—that entitled "Resistance to Civil Government," which was first published in Elizabeth Peabody's *Aesthetic Papers* in the spring of 1849; and that entitled "Civil Disobedience," which was first published in his *A Yankee in Canada, with Anti-Slavery and Reform Papers* (Boston: Ticknor & Fields, 1866), four years after his death. Except for numerous (but trivial) differences in capitalization and punctuation—which were probably editorial rather than authorial changes—they vary only in a few sentences. I have chosen the 1866 version as my text on the assumption that it was based on a corrected copy made by Thoreau, but I have indicated in my annotations all additions and deletions of words from the 1849 text.

I am grateful to Alfred A. Knopf, Inc., for permission to include in my introduction excerpts from my biography *The Days of Henry Thoreau* (New York, 1965) and to J. Golden Taylor and the Utah State University Press for permission to include excerpts from my "The Influence of Civil Disobedience" published in Professor Taylor's *The Western Thoreau Centenary* (Utah State University Press Monograph Series, X, 1963).

PART II

The Text

CIVIL DISOBEDIENCE[1]

I HEARTILY accept the motto,[2]—"That government is best which governs least"; and I should like to see it acted up to more rapidly and systematically. Carried out, it finally amounts to this, which also I believe,—"That government is best which governs not at all"; and when men are prepared for it, that will be the kind of government which they will have. Government is at best but an expedient; but most governments are usually, and all governments are sometimes, inexpedient. The objections which have been brought against a standing army, and they are many and weighty, and deserve to prevail, may also at last be brought against a standing government. The standing army is only an arm of the standing government. The government itself, which is only the mode which the people have chosen to execute their will, is equally liable to be abused and perverted before the people can act through it. Witness the present Mexican war,[3] the work of comparatively a few individuals using the standing government as their tool; for, in the outset, the people would not have consented to this measure.

This American government,—what is it but a tradition, though a recent one, endeavoring to transmit itself unimpaired to posterity, but each instant losing some of its integrity? It has not the vitality and force of a single living man; for a single man can bend it to his will. It is a sort of wooden gun to the people themselves.[4] But it is not the less necessary for this; for the people must have some complicated machinery or other, and hear its din, to satisfy that idea of government which they

31

have. Governments show thus how successfully men can be imposed on, even impose on themselves, for their own advantage. It is excellent, we must all allow. Yet this government never of itself furthered any enterprise, but by the alacrity with which it got out of its way. *It* does not keep the country free. *It* does not settle the West. *It* does not educate. The character inherent in the American people has done all that has been accomplished; and it would have done somewhat more, if the government had not sometimes got in its way. For government is an expedient by which men would fain succeed in letting one another alone; and, as has been said, when it is most expedient, the governed are most let alone by it. Trade and commerce, if they were not made of India-rubber, would never manage to bounce over the obstacles which legislators are continually putting in their way; and, if one were to judge these men wholly by the effects of their actions and not partly by their intentions, they would deserve to be classed and punished with those mischievous persons who put obstructions on the railroads.

But, to speak practically and as a citizen, unlike those who call themselves no-government men,[5] I ask for, not at once no government, but *at once* a better government. Let every man make known what kind of government would command his respect, and that will be one step toward obtaining it.

After all, the practical reason why, when the power is once in the hands of the people, a majority are permitted, and for a long period continue, to rule, is not because they are most likely to be in the right, nor because this seems fairest to the minority, but because they are physically the strongest. But a government in which the majority rule in all cases cannot be based on justice, even as far as men understand it. Can there not be a government in which majorities do not virtually decide right and wrong, but conscience?—in which majorities decide only those questions to which the rule of expediency is applicable? Must the citizen ever for a moment, or in the least degree, resign his conscience to the legislator? Why has every man a conscience.

32

then? I think that we should be men first, and subjects afterward. It is not desirable to cultivate a respect for the law, so much as for the right. The only obligation which I have a right to assume, is to do at any time what I think right. It is truly enough said, that a corporation has no conscience[6]; but a corporation of conscientious men is a corporation *with* a conscience. Law never made men a whit more just; and, by means of their respect for it, even the well-disposed are daily made the agents of injustice. A common and natural result of an undue respect for law is, that you may see a file of soldiers, colonel, captain, corporal, privates, powder-monkeys,[7] and all, marching in admirable order over hill and dale to the wars, against their wills, ay, against their common sense and consciences, which makes it very steep marching indeed, and produces a palpitation of the heart. They have no doubt that it is a damnable business in which they are concerned; they are all peaceably inclined. Now, what are they? Men at all? or small movable forts and magazines, at the service of some unscrupulous man in power? Visit the Navy-Yard, and behold a marine, such a man as an American government can make, or such as it can make a man with its black arts,—a mere shadow and reminiscence of humanity, a man laid out alive and standing, and already, as one may say, buried under arms with funeral accompaniments, though it may be,—

> "Not a drum was heard, not a funeral note,
> As his corse to the rampart we hurried;
> Not a soldier discharged his farewell shot
> O'er the grave where our hero we buried."[8]

The mass of men serve the state thus, not as men mainly, but as machines, with their bodies. They are the standing army, and the militia, jailers, constables, posse comitatus,[9]&c. In most cases there is no free exercise whatever of the judgment or of the moral sense; but they put themselves on a level with wood and earth and stones; and wooden men can perhaps be manufactured that will serve the purpose as well. Such command no more respect than men of straw or a lump of dirt. They have the same sort of worth only as horses and dogs. Yet such as these even are commonly esteemed good citizens. Others,—as most legislators, politicians, lawyers, ministers, and office-holders,—serve the state chiefly with their heads; and, as they rarely make any moral distinctions, they are as likely to serve the Devil, without *intending* it, as God. A very few, as heroes, patriots, martyrs, reformers in the great sense, and *men*, serve the state with their consciences also, and so necessarily resist it for the most part; and they are commonly treated as enemies by it. A wise man will only be useful as a man, and will not submit to be "clay," and "stop a hole to keep the wind away,"[10] but leave that office to his dust at least:—

> "I am too high-born to be propertied,
> To be a secondary at control,
> Or useful serving-man and instrument
> To any sovereign state throughout the world."[11]

He who gives himself entirely to his fellow-men appears to them useless and selfish; but he who gives himself partially to them is pronounced a benefactor and philanthropist.

How does it become a man to behave toward this American government to-day? I answer, that he cannot without disgrace be associated with it. I cannot for an instant recognize that political organization as *my* government which is the *slave's* government also.

All men recognize the right of revolution; that is, the right to refuse allegiance to, and to resist, the government, when its tyranny or its inefficiency are great and unendurable. But almost all say that such is not the case now. But such was the case, they think, in the Revolution of '75.[12] If one were to tell me that this was a bad government because it taxed certain foreign commodities brought to its ports, it is most probable that I should not make an ado about it, for I can do without them. All machines have their friction; and possibly this does enough good to counterbalance the evil. At any rate, it is a great evil to make a stir about it. But when the friction comes to have its machine, and oppression and robbery are organized, I say, let us not have such a machine any longer. In other words, when a sixth of the population of a nation which has undertaken to be the refuge of liberty are slaves, and a whole country is unjustly overrun and conquered by a foreign army, and subjected to military law, I think that it is not too soon for honest men to rebel and revolutionize. What makes this duty the more urgent is the fact, that the country so overrun is not our own, but ours is the invading army.

Paley,[13] a common authority with many on moral questions, in his chapter on the "Duty of Submission to Civil Government," resolves all civil obligation into expediency; and he proceeds to say, "that so long as the interest of the whole society requires it, that is, so long as the established government cannot be resisted or changed without public inconveniency, it is the will of God that the established government be obeyed, and no longer. . . . This principle being admitted, the justice of every particular case of resistance is reduced to a computation of the quantity of the danger and grievance on the one side, and of the probability and expense of redressing it on the other." Of this, he says, every man shall judge for himself. But Paley appears never to have contemplated those cases to which the rule of expediency does not apply, in which a people, as well as an individual, must do justice, cost what it may. If I have unjustly wrested a plank from a drowning man, I must restore it to him though I drown myself.[14] This, according to Paley, would be inconvenient. But he that would save his life, in such a case, shall lose it[15] This people must cease to hold slaves, and to make war on Mexico, though it cost them their existence as a people.

In their practice, nations agree with Paley; but does any one think that Massachusetts does exactly what is right at the present crisis?

"A drab of state, a cloth-o'-silver slut,
  To have her train borne up, and her soul trail in the dirt."[16]

Practically speaking, the opponents to a reform in Massachusetts are not a hundred thousand politicians at the South, but a hundred thousand merchants and farmers here,[17] who are more interested in commerce and agriculture than they are in humanity, and are not prepared to do justice to the slave and to Mexico, *cost what it may.* I quarrel not with far-off foes, but with those who, near at home, co-operate with, and do the bidding of, those far away, and without whom the latter would be harmless. We are accustomed to say, that the mass of men are unprepared; but improvement is slow, because the few are not materially wiser or better than the many. It is not so important that many should be as good as you, as that there be some absolute goodness somewhere; for that will leaven the whole lump.[18] There are thousands who are *in opinion* opposed to slavery and to the war, who yet in effect do nothing to put an end to them; who, esteeming themselves children of Washington and Franklin, sit down with their hands in their pockets, and say that they know not what to do, and do nothing; who even postpone the question of freedom to the question of free-trade, and quietly read the prices-current along with the latest advices from Mexico, after dinner, and, it may be, fall asleep over them both. What is the price-current of an honest man and patriot to-day? They hesitate, and they regret, and sometimes they petition; but they do nothing in earnest and with effect. They will wait, well disposed, for others to remedy the evil, that they may no longer have it to regret. At most, they give only a cheap vote, and a feeble countenance and God-speed, to the right, as it goes by them. There are nine hundred and ninety-nine patrons of virtue to one virtuous man. But it is easier to deal with the real possessor of a thing than with the temporary guardian of it.

All voting is a sort of gaming, like checkers or backgammon, with a slight moral tinge to it, a playing with right and wrong, with moral questions; and betting naturally accompanies it. The character of the voters is not staked. I cast my vote, perchance, as I think right; but I am not vitally concerned that that right should prevail. I am willing to leave it to the majority. Its obligation, therefore, never exceeds that of expediency. Even voting *for the right* is *doing* nothing for it. It is only expressing to men feebly your desire that it should prevail. A wise man will not leave the right to the mercy of chance, nor wish it to prevail through the power of the majority. There is but little virtue in the action of masses of men. When the majority shall at length vote for the abolition of slavery, it will be because they are indifferent to slavery, or because there is but little slavery left to be abolished by their vote. *They* will then be the only slaves. Only *his* vote can hasten the abolition of slavery who asserts his own freedom by his vote.

I hear of a convention to be held at Baltimore,[19] or elsewhere, for the selection of a candidate for the Presidency, made up chiefly of editors, and men who are politicians by profession; but I think, what is it to any independent, intelligent, and respectable man what decision they may come to? Shall we not have the advantage of his wisdom and honesty, nevertheless? Can we not count upon some independent votes? Are there not many individuals in the country who do not attend conventions? But no: I find that the respectable man, so called, has immediately drifted from his position, and despairs of his country, when his country has more reason to despair of him. He forthwith adopts one of the candidates thus selected as the only *available* one, thus proving that he is himself *available* for any purposes of the demagogue. His vote is of no more worth than that of any unprincipled foreigner or hireling native, who may have been bought. O for a man who is a *man,* and, as my neighbor says, has a bone in his back which you cannot pass your hand through! Our statistics are at fault: the population has been returned too large. How many *men* are there to a square thousand miles in this country? Hardly one. Does not America offer any inducement for men to settle here? The American has dwindled into an Odd Fellow,[20]—one who may be known by the development of his organ of gregariousness, and a manifest lack of intellect and cheerful self-reliance;[21] whose first and chief concern, on coming into the world, is to see that the Almshouses are in good repair; and, before yet he has lawfully donned the virile garb,[22] to collect a fund for the support of the widows and orphans that may be; who, in short, ventures to live only by the aid of the Mutual Insurance Company, which has promised to bury him decently.

It is not a man's duty, as a matter of course, to devote himself to the eradication of any, even the most enormous wrong; he may still properly have other concerns to engage him; but it is his duty, at least, to wash his hands of it, and, if he gives it no thought longer, not to give it practically his support. If I devote myself to other pursuits and contemplations, I must first see, at least, that I do not pursue them sitting upon another man's shoulders. I must get off him first, that he may pursue his contemplations too. See what gross inconsistency is tolerated. I have heard some of my townsmen say, "I should like to have them order me out to help put down an insurrection of the slaves, or to march to Mexico;—see if I would go"; and yet these very men have each, directly by their allegiance, and so indirectly, at least, by their money, furnished a substitute. The soldier is applauded who refuses to serve in an unjust war by those who do not refuse to sustain the unjust government which makes the war; is applauded by those whose own act and authority he disregards and sets at naught; as if the State were penitent to that degree that it hired one to scourge it while it sinned, but not to that degree that it left off sinning for a moment. Thus, under the name of Order and Civil Government, we are all made at last to pay homage to and support our own meanness. After the first blush of sin comes its indifference; and from immoral it becomes, as it were, *un*moral, and not quite unnecessary to that life which we have made.

The broadest and most prevalent error requires the most disinterested virtue to sustain it. The slight reproach to which the virtue of patriotism is commonly liable, the noble are most likely to incur. Those who, while they disapprove of the character and measures of a government, yield to it their allegiance and support, are undoubtedly its most conscientious supporters, and so frequently the most serious obstacles to reform. Some are petitioning[23] the State to dissolve the Union, to disregard the requisitions of the President. Why do they not dissolve it themselves,—the union between themselves and the State,—and refuse to pay their quota into its treasury? Do not they stand in the same relation to the State, that the State does to the Union? And have not the same reasons prevented the State from resisting the Union, which have prevented them from resisting the State?

How can a man be satisfied to entertain an opinion merely, and enjoy *it?* Is there any enjoyment in it, if his opinion is that he is aggrieved? If you are cheated out of a single dollar by your neighbor, you do not rest satisfied with knowing that you are cheated, or with saying that you are cheated, or even with petitioning him to pay you your due; but you take effectual steps at once to obtain the full amount, and see that you are never cheated again. Action from principle, the perception and the performance of right, changes things and relations; it is essentially revolutionary, and does not consist wholly with anything which was. It not only divides states and churches, it divides families; ay, it divides the *individual,* separating the diabolical in him from the divine.

Unjust laws exist: shall we be content to obey them, or shall we endeavor to amend them, and obey them until we have succeeded, or shall we transgress them at once? Men generally, under such a government as this, think that they ought to wait until they have persuaded the majority to alter them. They think that, if they should resist, the remedy would be worse than the evil. But it is the fault of the government itself that the remedy *is* worse than the evil. *It* makes it worse. Why is it not more apt to anticipate and provide for reform? Why does it not cherish its wise minority? Why does it cry and resist before it is hurt? Why does it not encourage its citizens to be on the alert to point out its faults, and *do* better than it would have them? Why does it always crucify Christ, and excommunicate Copernicus[24] and Luther,[25] and pronounce Washington and Franklin[26] rebels?

One would think, that a deliberate and practical denial of its authority was the only offence never contemplated by government; else, why has it not assigned its definite, its suitable and proportionate penalty? If a man who has no property refuses but once to earn nine shillings for the State, he is put in prison for a period unlimited by any law that I know, and determined only by the discretion of those who placed him there; but if he should steal ninety times nine shillings from the State, he is soon permitted to go at large again.

If the injustice is part of the necessary friction of the machine of government, let it go, let it go: perchance it will wear smooth,—certainly the machine will wear out. If the injustice has a spring, or a pulley, or a rope, or a crank, exclusively for itself, then perhaps you may consider whether the remedy will not be worse than the evil; but if it is of such a nature that it requires you to be the agent of injustice to another, then, I say, break the law. Let your life be a counter friction to stop the machine. What I have to do is to see, at any rate, that I do not lend myself to the wrong which I condemn.

As for adopting the ways which the State has provided for remedying the evil, I know not of such ways. They take too much time, and a man's life will be gone. I have other affairs to attend to. I came into this world, not chiefly to make this a good place to live in, but to live in it, be it good or bad. A man has not everything to do, but something; and because he cannot do *everything*, it is not necessary that he should do *something* wrong. It is not my business to be petitioning the Governor or the Legislature any more than it is theirs to petition me; and, if they should not hear my petition, what should I do then? But in this case the State has provided no way: its very Constitution is the evil. This may seem to be harsh and stubborn and unconciliatory; but it is to treat with the utmost kindness and consideration the only spirit that can appreciate or deserves it. So is all change for the better, like birth and death, which convulse the body.

I do not hesitate to say, that those who call themselves Abolitionists should at once effectually withdraw their support, both in person and property, from the government of Massachusetts, and not wait till they constitute a majority of one, before they suffer the right to prevail through them. I think that it is enough if they have God on their side, without waiting for that other one. Moreover, any man more right than his neighbors constitutes a majority of one already.[27]

I meet this American government, or its representative, the State government, directly, and face to face, once a year—no more—in the person of its tax-gatherer; this is the only mode in which a man situated as I am necessarily meets it; and it then says distinctly, Recognize me; and the simplest, the most effectual, and, in the present posture of affairs, the indispensablest mode of treating with it on this head, of expressing your little satisfaction with and love for it, is to deny it then. My civil neighbor, the tax-gatherer, is the very man I have to deal with,—for it is, after all, with men and not with parchment that I quarrel,—and he has voluntarily chosen to be an agent of the government. How shall he ever know well what he is and does as an officer of the government, or as a man, until he is obliged to consider whether he shall treat me, his neighbor, for whom he has respect, as a neighbor and well-disposed man, or as a maniac and disturber of the peace, and see if he can get over this obstruction to his neighborliness without a ruder and more impetuous thought or speech corresponding with his action. I know this well, that if one thousand, if one hundred, if ten men whom I could name,—if ten *honest* men only,—ay, if *one* HONEST man, in this State of Massachusetts, *ceasing to hold slaves*, were actually to withdraw from this copartnership, and be locked up in the county jail therefor, it would be the abolition of slavery in America. For it matters not how small the beginning may seem to be: what is once well done is done forever. But we love better to talk about it: that we say is our mission. Reform keeps many scores of newspapers in its service, but not one man. If my esteemed neighbor, the State's ambassador,[28] who will devote his days to the settlement of the question of human rights in the Council Chamber, instead of being threatened with the prisons of Carolina, were to sit down the prisoner of Massachusetts, that State which is so anxious to foist the sin of slavery upon her sister,—though at present she can discover only an act of inhospitality to be the ground of a quarrel with her,—the Legislature would not wholly waive the subject the following winter.

Under a government which imprisons any unjustly, the true place for a just man is also a prison. The proper place to-day, the only place which Massachusetts has provided for her freer and less desponding spirits, is in her prisons, to be put out and locked out of the State by her own act, as they have already put themselves out by their principles. It is there that the fugitive slave, and the Mexican prisoner on parole, and the Indian[29] come to plead the wrongs of his race, should find them; on that separate, but more free and honorable ground, where the State places those who are not *with* her, but *against* her,— the only house in a slave State in which a free man can abide with honor. If any think that their influence would be lost there, and their voices no longer afflict the ear of the State, that they would not be as an enemy within its walls, they do not know by how much truth is stronger than error, nor how much more eloquently and effectively he can combat injustice who has experienced a little in his own person. Cast your whole vote, not a strip of paper merely, but your whole influence. A minority is powerless while it conforms to the majority; it is not even a minority then; but it is irresistible when it clogs by its whole weight. If the alternative is to keep all just men in prison, or give up war and slavery, the State will not hesitate which to choose. If a thousand men were not to pay their tax-bills this year, that would not be a violent and bloody measure, as it would be to pay them, and enable the State to commit violence and shed innocent blood. This is, in fact, the definition of a peaceable revolution, if any such is possible. If the tax-gatherer, or any other public officer, asks me, as one has done, "But what shall I do?" my answer is, "If you really wish to do anything, resign your office." When the subject has refused allegiance, and the officer has resigned his office, then the revolution is accomplished. But even suppose blood should flow. Is there not a sort of blood shed when the conscience is wounded? Through this wound a man's real manhood and immortality flow out, and he bleeds to an everlasting death. I see this blood flowing now.

I have contemplated the imprisonment of the offender, rather than the seizure of his goods,—though both will serve the same purpose,—because they who assert the purest right, and consequently are most dangerous to a corrupt State, commonly have not spent much time in accumulating property. To such the State renders comparatively small service, and a slight tax is wont to appear exorbitant, particularly if they are obliged to earn it by special labor with their hands. If there were one who lived wholly without the use of money,[30] the State itself would hesitate to demand it of him. But the rich man,—not to make any invidious comparison,—is always sold to the institution which makes him rich. Absolutely speaking, the more money, the less virtue; for money comes between a man and his objects, and obtains them for him; and it was certainly no great virtue to obtain it. It puts to rest many questions which he would otherwise be taxed to answer; while the only new question which it puts is the hard but superfluous one, how to spend it. Thus his moral ground is taken from under his feet. The opportunities of living are diminished in proportion as what are called the "means" are increased. The best thing a man can do for his culture when he is rich is to endeavor to carry out those schemes which he entertained when he was poor. Christ answered the Herodians according to their condition. "Show me the tribute-money," said he;—and one took a penny out of his pocket;—if you use money which has the image of Caesar on it, and which he has made current and valuable, that is, *if you are men of the State,* and gladly enjoy the advantages of Caesar's government, then pay him back some of his own when he demands it; "Render therefore to Caesar that which is Caesar's, and to God those things which are God's,"[31]—leaving them no wiser than before as to which was which; for they did not wish to know.

When I converse with the freest of my neighbors, I perceive that, whatever they may say about the magnitude and seriousness of the question, and their regard for the public tranquillity, the long and the short of the matter is, that they cannot spare the protection of the existing government, and they dread the consequences to their property and families of disobedience to it.[32] For my own part, I should not like to think that I ever rely on the protection of the State. But, if I deny the authority of the State when it presents its tax-bill, it will soon take and waste all my property, and so harass me and my children without end. This is hard. This makes it impossible for a man to live honestly, and at the same time comfortably, in outward respects. It will not be worth the while to accumulate property; that would be sure to go again. You must hire or squat somewhere, and raise but a small crop, and eat that soon. You must live within yourself, and depend upon yourself always tucked up and ready for a start, and not have many affairs. A man may grow rich in Turkey even, if he will be in all respects a good subject of the Turkish government. Confucius said: "If a state is governed by the principles of reason, poverty and misery are subjects of shame; if a state is not governed by the principles of reason, riches and honors are the subjects of shame."[33] No; until I want the protection of Massachusetts to be extended to me in some distant Southern port, where my liberty is endangered, or until I am bent solely on building up an estate at home by peaceful enterprise, I can afford to refuse allegiance to Massachusetts, and her right to my property and life. It costs me less in every sense to incur the penalty of disobedience to the State, than it would to obey. I should feel as if I were worth less in that case.

Some years ago, the State met me in behalf of the Church,[34] and commanded me to pay a certain sum toward the support of a clergyman whose preaching my father attended, but never I myself. "Pay," it said, "or be locked up in the jail." I declined to pay. But, unfortunately, another man saw fit to pay it. I did not see why the schoolmaster should be taxed to support the priest, and not the priest the schoolmaster; for I was not the State's schoolmaster, but I supported myself by voluntary subscription. I did not see why the lyceum[35] should not present its tax-bill, and have the State to back its demand, as well as the Church. However, at the request of the selectmen, I condescended to make some such statement as this in writing:— "Know all men by these presents, that I, Henry Thoreau, do not wish to be regarded as a member of any incorporated society which I have not joined." This I gave to the town clerk; and he has it. The State, having thus learned that I did not wish to be regarded as a member of that church, has never made a like demand on me since; though it said that it must adhere to its original presumption that time. If I had known how to name them, I should then have signed off in detail from all the societies which I never signed on to; but I did not know where to find a complete list.

I have paid no poll-tax for six years. I was put into a jail once on this account, for one night;[36] and, as I stood considering the walls of solid stone,[37] two or three feet thick, the door of wood and iron, a foot thick, and the iron grating which strained the light, I could not help being struck with the foolishness of that institution which treated me as if I were

45

mere flesh and blood and bones, to be locked up. I won-
dered that it should have concluded at length that this was the
best use it could put me to, and had never thought to avail itself
of my services in some way. I saw that, if there was a wall of
stone between me and my townsmen, there was a still more
difficult one to climb or break through, before they could get
to be as free as I was. I did not for a moment feel confined,
and the walls seemed a great waste of stone and mortar. I felt
as if I alone of all my townsmen had paid my tax. They plainly
did not know how to treat me, but behaved like persons who are
underbred. In every threat and in every compliment there was
a blunder; for they thought that my chief desire was to stand
the other side of that stone wall. I could not but smile to see
how industriously they locked the door on my meditations,
which followed them out again without let or hindrance, and
they were really all that was dangerous. As they could not reach
me, they had resolved to punish my body; just as boys, if they
cannot come at some person against whom they have a spite,
will abuse his dog. I saw that the State was half-witted, that it
was timid as a lone woman with her silver spoons, and that it
did not know its friends from its foes, and I lost all my remain-
ing respect for it, and pitied it.

Thus the State never intentionally confronts a man's sense,
intellectual or moral, but only his body, his senses. It is not
armed with superior wit or honesty, but with superior physical
strength. I was not born to be forced. I will breathe after my
own fashion. Let us see who is the strongest. What force has
a multitude? They only can force me who obey a higher law[38]
than I. They force me to become like themselves. I do not hear
of *men* being *forced* to live this way or that by masses of men.
What sort of life were that to live? When I meet a government
which says to me, "Your money or your life," why should I be
in haste to give it my money? It may be in a great strait, and
not know what to do: I cannot help that. It must help itself; do
as I do. It is not worth the while to snivel about it. I am not

responsible for the successful working of the machinery of society. I am not the son of the engineer. I perceive that, when an acorn and a chestnut fall side by side, the one does not remain inert to make way for the other, but both obey their own laws, and spring and grow and flourish as best they can, till one, perchance, overshadows and destroys the other. If a plant cannot live according to its nature, it dies; and so a man.

The night in prison was novel and interesting enough. The prisoners in their shirt-sleeves were enjoying a chat and the evening air in the doorway, when I entered. But the jailer[39] said, "Come, boys, it is time to lock up"; and so they dispersed, and I heard the sound of their steps returning into the hollow apartments. My room-mate was introduced to me by the jailer, as "a first-rate fellow and a clever man." When the door was locked, he showed me where to hang my hat, and how he managed matters there. The rooms were whitewashed once a month; and this one, at least, was the whitest, most simply furnished, and probably the neatest apartment in the town. He naturally wanted to know where I came from, and what brought me there; and, when I had told him, I asked him in my turn how he came there, presuming him to be an honest man, of course; and, as the world goes, I believe he was. "Why," said he, "they accuse me of burning a barn; but I never did it." As near as I could discover, he had probably gone to bed in a barn when drunk, and smoked his pipe there; and so a barn was burnt. He had the reputation of being a clever man, had been there some three months waiting for his trial[40] to come on, and would have to wait as much longer; but he was quite domesticated and contented, since he got his board for nothing, and thought that he was well treated.

He occupied one window, and I the other; and I saw, that, if one stayed there long, his principal business would be to look out the window. I had soon read all the tracts that were left there, and examined where former prisoners had broken out,

47

and where a grate had been sawed off, and heard the history of the various occupants of that room; for I found that even here there was a history and a gossip which never circulated beyond the walls of the jail. Probably this is the only house in the town where verses are composed, which are afterward printed in a circular form, but not published. I was shown quite a long list of verses which were composed by some young men who had been detected in an attempt to escape, who avenged themselves by singing them.

I pumped my fellow-prisoner as dry as I could, for fear I should never see him again; but at length he showed me which was my bed, and left me to blow out the lamp.

It was like travelling into a far country, such as I had never expected to behold, to lie there for one night. It seemed to me that I never had heard the town-clock strike before, nor the evening sounds of the village; for we slept with the windows open, which were inside the grating. It was to see my native village in the light of the Middle Ages, and our Concord was turned into a Rhine stream, and visions of knights and castles passed before me. They were the voices of old burghers that I heard in the streets. I was an involuntary spectator and auditor of whatever was done and said in the kitchen of the adjacent village-inn,[41]—a wholly new and rare experience to me. It was a closer view of my native town. I was fairly inside of it. I never had seen its institutions before. This is one of its peculiar institutions; for it is a shire town.[42] I began to comprehend what its inhabitants were about.

In the morning, our breakfasts were put through the hole in the door, in small oblong-square tin pans, made to fit, and holding a pint of chocolate, with brown bread, and an iron spoon. When they called for the vessels again, I was green enough to return what bread I had left; but my comrade seized it, and said that I should lay that up for lunch or dinner. Soon after he was let out to work at haying in a neighboring field, whither he went every day, and would not be back till noon; so he bade me good-day, saying that he doubted if he should see me again.

When I came out of prison,—for some one[43] interfered, and paid that tax,—I did not perceive that great changes had taken place on the common, such as he observed who went in a youth, and emerged a tottering and gray-headed man; and yet a change had to my eyes come over the scene,—the town, and State, and country,—greater than any that mere time could effect. I saw yet more distinctly the State in which I lived. I saw to what extent the people among whom I lived could be trusted as good neighbors and friends; that their friendship was for summer weather only;[44] that they did not greatly propose to do right; that they were a distinct race from me by their prejudices and superstitions, as the Chinamen and Malays are; that, in their sacrifices to humanity, they ran no risks, not even to their property; that, after all, they were not so noble but they treated the thief as he had treated them, and hoped, by a certain outward observance and a few prayers, and by walking in a particular straight though useless path[45] from time to time, to save their souls. This may be to judge my neighbors harshly; for I believe that many of them are not aware that they have such an institution as the jail in their village.

It was formerly the custom in our village, when a poor debtor came out of jail, for his acquaintances to salute him, looking through their fingers, which were crossed to represent the grating of a jail window, "How do ye do?" My neighbors did not thus salute me, but first looked at me, and then at one another, as if I had returned from a long journey.[46] I was put into jail as I was going to the shoemaker's to get a shoe which was mended. When I was let out the next morning, I proceeded to finish my errand, and having put on my mended shoe, joined a huckleberry party, who were impatient to put themselves under my conduct; and in half an hour,—for the horse was soon tackled,—was in the midst of a huckleberry field, on one of our highest hills, two miles off, and then the State was nowhere to be seen.

This is the whole history of "My Prisons."[47]

I have never declined paying the highway tax, because I am as desirous of being a good neighbor as I am of being a bad subject; and, as for supporting schools, I am doing my part to educate my fellow-countrymen now. It is for no particular item in the tax-bill that I refuse to pay it. I simply wish to refuse allegiance to the State, to withdraw and stand aloof from it effectually. I do not care to trace the course of my dollar, if I could, till it buys a man or a musket to shoot one with,—the dollar is innocent,—but I am concerned to trace the effects of my allegiance. In fact, I quietly declare war with the State, after my fashion, though I will still make what use and get what advantage of her I can, as is usual in such cases.

If others pay the tax which is demanded of me, from a sympathy with the State, they do but what they have already done in their own case, or rather they abet injustice to a greater extent than the State requires. If they pay the tax from a mistaken interest in the individual taxed, to save his property, or prevent his going to jail, it is because they have not considered wisely how far they let their private feelings interfere with the public good.

This, then, is my position at present. But one cannot be too much on his guard in such a case, lest his action be biassed by obstinacy, or an undue regard for the opinions of men. Let him see that he does only what belongs to himself and to the hour.

I think sometimes, Why, this people mean well; they are only ignorant; they would do better if they knew how: why give your neighbors this pain to treat you as they are not inclined to? But I think again, this is no reason why I should do as they do, or permit others to suffer much greater pain of a different kind. Again, I sometimes say to myself, When many millions of men, without heat, without ill will, without personal feeling of any kind, demand of you a few shillings only, without the possibility, such is their constitution, of retracting or altering their present demand, and without the possibility, on your side, of appeal to any other millions, why expose yourself to this overwhelming brute force? You do not resist cold and hunger, the winds and the waves, thus obstinately; you quietly submit to a thousand similar necessities. You do not put your head into the fire. But just in proportion as I regard this as not wholly a brute force, but partly a human force, and consider that I have relations to those millions as to so many millions of men, and not of mere brute or inanimate things, I see that appeal is possible, first and instantaneously, from them to the Maker of them, and, secondly, from them to themselves. But, if I put my head deliberately into the fire, there is no appeal to fire or to the Maker of fire, and I have only myself to blame. If I could convince myself that I have any right to be satisfied with men as they are, and to treat them accordingly, and not according, in some respects, to my requisitions and expectations of what they and I ought to be, then, like a good Mussulman[48] and fatalist, I should endeavor to be satisfied with things as they are, and say it is the will of God. And, above all, there is this difference between resisting this and a purely brute or natural force, that I can resist this with some effect; but I cannot expect, like Orpheus,[49] to change the nature of the rocks and trees and beasts.

I do not wish to quarrel with any man or nation. I do not wish to split hairs, to make fine distinctions, or set myself up as better than my neighbors. I seek rather, I may say, even an excuse for conforming to the laws of the land. I am but too ready to conform to them. Indeed, I have reason to suspect myself on this head; and each year, as the tax-gatherer comes round, I find myself disposed to review the acts and position of the general and State governments, and the spirit of the people, to discover a pretext for conformity.

"We must affect our country as our parents;
And if at any time we alienate
Our love or industry from doing it honor,
We must respect effects and teach the soul
Matter of conscience and religion,
And not desire of rule or benefit."[50]

I believe that the State will soon be able to take all my work of this sort out of my hands, and then I shall be no better a patriot than my fellow-countrymen. Seen from a lower point of view, the Constitution, with all its faults, is very good; the law and the courts are very respectable; even this State and this American government are, in many respects, very admirable and rare things, to be thankful for, such as a great many have described them; but seen from a point of view a little higher, they are what I have described them; seen from a higher still, and the highest, who shall say what they are, or that they are worth looking at or thinking of at all?

However, the government does not concern me much, and I shall bestow the fewest possible thoughts on it. It is not many moments that I live under a government, even in this world. If a man is thought-free, fancy-free, imagination-free, that which *is not* never for a long time appearing *to be* to him, unwise rulers or reformers cannot fatally interrupt him.

I know that most men think differently from myself; but those whose lives are by profession devoted to the study of these or kindred subjects, content me as little as any. Statesmen and legislators, standing so completely within the institution, never distinctly and nakedly behold it. They speak of moving society, but have no resting-place without it. They may be men of a certain experience and discrimination, and have no doubt invented ingenious and even useful systems, for which we sincerely thank them; but all their wit and usefulness lie within certain not very wide limits. They are wont to forget that the world is not governed by policy and expediency. Webster[51] never goes behind government, and so cannot speak with authority about it. His words are wisdom to those legislators who contemplate no essential reform in the existing government; but for thinkers, and those who legislate for all time, he never once glances at the subject. I know of those whose serene and wise speculations on this theme would soon reveal the limits of his mind's range and hospitality. Yet, compared with the cheap professions of most reformers, and the still cheaper wisdom and eloquence of politicians in general, his are almost the only sensible and valuable words, and we thank Heaven for him. Comparatively, he is always strong, original, and, above all, practical. Still his quality is not wisdom, but prudence. The lawyer's truth is not Truth, but consistency, or a consistent expediency. Truth is always in harmony with herself, and is not concerned chiefly to reveal the justice that may consist with wrong-doing. He well deserves to be called, as he has been called, the Defender of the Constitution. There are really no blows to be given by him but defensive ones. He is not a leader, but a follower. His leaders are the men of '87.[52] "I have never made an effort," he says, "and never propose to make an effort; I have never countenanced an effort, and never mean to countenance an effort, to disturb the arrangement as originally made, by which the various States came into the Union."[53] Still thinking of the sanction which the Constitution gives to slavery, he says, "Because it was a part of the original compact,—let it stand." Notwithstanding his special acuteness and ability, he is unable to take a fact out of its merely political relations, and behold it as it lies absolutely to be disposed of by the intellect,—what, for instance, it behooves a man to do here in America to-day with regard to slavery, but ventures, or is driven, to make some such desperate answer as the following, while professing to speak absolutely, and as a private man,—from which what new and singular code of social duties might be inferred? "The manner," says he, "in which the governments of those States where slavery exists are to regulate it, is for their own consideration, under their responsibility to their constituents, to the general laws of propriety, humanity, and justice, and to God. Associations formed elsewhere, springing from a feeling of humanity, or any other cause, have nothing whatever to do with it. They have never received any encouragement from me, and they never will."*[54]

They who know of no purer sources of truth, who have traced up its stream no higher, stand, and wisely stand, by the Bible and the Constitution, and drink at it there with reverence and humility; but they who behold where it comes trickling into this lake or that pool, gird up their loins once more,[55] and continue their pilgrimage toward its fountain-head.

No man with a genius for legislation has appeared in America. They are rare in the history of the world. There are orators, politicians, and eloquent men, by the thousand; but the speaker has not yet opened his mouth to speak, who is capable of settling the much-vexed questions of the day. We love eloquence for its own sake, and not for any truth which it may utter, or any heroism it may inspire. Our legislators have not yet learned the comparative value of free-trade and of freedom, of union, and of rectitude, to a nation. They have no genius or talent for comparatively humble questions of taxation and finance, commerce and manufactures and agriculture. If we were left solely to the wordy wit of legislators in Congress for our guidance, uncorrected by the seasonable experience and the effectual complaints of the people, America would not long retain her rank among the nations. For eighteen hundred years, though perchance I have no right to say it, the New Testament has been written; yet where is the legislator who has wisdom and practical

---

* These extracts have been inserted since the Lecture was read. [Thoreau's Footnote.]

54

talent enough to avail himself of the light which it sheds on the science of legislation?

The authority of government, even such as I am willing to submit to,—for I will cheerfully obey those who know and can do better than I, and in many things even those who neither know nor can do so well,—is still an impure one: to be strictly just, it must have the sanction and consent of the governed. It can have no pure right over my person and property but what I concede to it. The progress from an absolute to a limited monarchy, from a limited monarchy to a democracy, is a progress toward a true respect for the individual. Even the Chinese philosopher was wise enough to regard the individual as the basis of the empire.[56] Is a democracy, such as we know it, the last improvement possible in government? Is it not possible to take a step further towards recognizing and organizing the rights of man? There will never be a really free and enlightened State, until the State comes to recognize the individual as a higher and independent power, from which all its own power and authority are derived, and treats him accordingly. I please myself with imagining a State at last which can afford to be just to all men, and to treat the individual with respect as a neighbor; which even would not think it inconsistent with its own repose, if a few were to live aloof from it, not meddling with it, nor embraced by it, who fulfilled all the duties of neighbors and fellow-men. A State which bore this kind of fruit, and suffered it to drop off as fast as it ripened, would prepare the way for a still more perfect and glorious State, which also I have imagined, but not yet anywhere seen.[57]

PART III

Commentary

NOTES

1. When Thoreau first delivered the essay as a lecture before the Concord Lyceum on January 26, 1848, he entitled it "On the Relation of the Individual to the State." When it was first printed, in Elizabeth Peabody's *Aesthetic Papers* in May, 1849, it was entitled "Resistance to Civil Government." It did not receive its present title of "Civil Disobedience" until it was published in Thoreau's *A Yankee in Canada, with Anti-Slavery and Reform Papers* in 1866, four years after his death. Professor Tokihiko Yamasaki of Osaka City University has pointed out to me the pun in the title—not only does it imply disobedience of civil authority, but also a civil (*i.e.*, a courteous) form of disobedience.

2. The motto is not from Thomas Jefferson, as many have supposed, but is rather from the masthead of the *Democratic Review*, a periodical to which Thoreau several times contributed articles. (Lee A. Pederson, "Thoreau's Source of the Motto in 'Civil Disobedience, ' " *Thoreau Society Bulletin*, 67.)

3. The war with Mexico was not declared until 1846, whereas Thoreau had refused to pay his tax as early as 1843. In citing the war, he was simply taking advantage of the fact that the war was a particularly unpopular one in the North. (John C. Broderick, "Thoreau, Alcott, and the Poll Tax," *Studies in Philology*, LIII, 1956, 612-26.)

4. The *Aesthetic Papers* version at this point adds: "and, if ever they should use it in earnest as a real one against each other, it will surely split."

5. The 1840's, when "Civil Disobedience" was written, was a period of intense interest in social reform in the United States, which included a number of philosophical anarchists who advocated the dissolution of all government.

6. Thoreau is apparently thinking of Sir Edward Coke's "Corporations . . . have no souls" from his *Case of Sutton's Hospital.*

7. Those who transport gunpowder from the magazines to the guns during battle.

8. Charles Wolfe (1791-1823), "Burial of Sir John Moore at Corunna."

9. The entire body of inhabitants who may be summoned by the police in the event of a riot.

10. "Imperious Caesar, dead and turn'd to clay, Might stop a hole to keep the wind away."—Shakespeare, *Hamlet*, V. i. 236-37.

11. Shakespeare, *King John*, V. ii. 79-82.

12. The American Revolution, which began in Concord on April 19, 1775.

13. William Paley (1743-1805), *Moral and Political Philosophy*, VI. ii.

14. "If a fool should snatch a plank from a wreck, shall a wise man wrest it from him if he is able?"—Cicero, *De officiis*, III. xxiii.

15. "Whosoever will save his life shall lose it."—Matt. x: 39.

16. Cyril Tourneur, *The Revengers Tragaedie* (1608), IV. iv.

17. Much of the resistance against the abolition of slavery at the time came from northerners who feared that such a move would damage the economy of the nation and cut their own profits.

18. "Know ye not that a little leaven leaventh the whole lump?"—I Cor. v. 6.

19. The Democratic Party held its 1848 convention in Baltimore. Trying to walk the fence between North and South, they avoided any discussion of slavery.

20. The Independent Order of Odd Fellows is a secret fraternal order which still exists throughout the United States.

21. An allusion to Ralph Waldo Emerson's famous essay of that name.

22. Roman boys assumed the *toga virilis* upon attaining puberty.

23. Some of the more radical Abolitionists, believing that it would be impossible ever to force the abolition of slavery through Congress, advocated the Northern states' withdrawal from the Union rather than obedience to laws which endorsed slavery.

24. Nicolaus Copernicus (1473-1543) escaped excommunication for the dissertation on the solar system only because he was on his deathbed when it was published.

25. Martin Luther (1483-1546) was excommunicated by Pope Leo X in 1520.

26. Washington and Franklin were, of course, leaders of the American Revolution against British authority.

27. *Cf.*, "A Man with God is always in the majority"—John Knox (1505-72).

28. Samuel Hoar (1778-1856), Thoreau's neighbor and father of his close friend Edward Hoar, was sent to South Carolina by the Commonwealth of Massachusetts in 1844 to protest the arrest of Negro seamen on Massachusetts ships in South Carolina waters. He was forcibly evicted from the state by action of its legislature.

29. Thoreau was one of the few in his day to protest the ruthless treatment of the American Indian.

30. Edward Palmer, one of Thoreau's contemporaries, renounced the use of money entirely, and tried to pay his living costs with copies of the *Herald of Holiness*, a little paper he printed on New York's Bowery.

31. Matt. xxii : 19-21.

32. The word order of this sentence has been slightly changed from that of the *Aesthetic Papers* version.

33. *The Analects*. VIII. xiii.

34. In Thoreau's day, the church taxed each member of its congregation, and the taxes were billed and collected by the town officials. The First Parish Church (Unitarian) of Concord assumed that since Thoreau's parents attended the church, he himself wished to be considered a member and accordingly had him sent a tax bill in 1840. Because of his protest the bill was never sent again.

35. The lyceum movement sponsored lecture series in many American towns in the period from 1830 to the Civil War. Thoreau not only lectured frequently from their platform both in Concord and elsewhere, but was for a time curator of the Concord Lyceum.

36. It is not certain now just what night Thoreau did spend in the Concord jail, but it was probably either the 23rd or 24th of July, 1846.

37. The Concord jail was not a small-town lockup, but the Middlesex County Jail, a massive granite structure three stories high.

38. A favorite phrase with the Transcendentalists, referring to

one's conscience or "the voice of God within." Thoreau had a chapter by this title in *Walden*.

39. The local jailer, constable, and tax collector at the time was Sam Staples, a personal friend of Thoreau. In later years Thoreau often hired Staples as an assistant when he did surveying.

40. Thoreau later learned that his cellmate was acquitted when he came up for trial.

41. The Middlesex Hotel, no longer extant.

42. At that time Concord shared with Cambridge the honor of being county seat of Middlesex County.

43. Although the person who paid Thoreau's tax has never been positively identified, it is generally agreed that it was probably his Aunt Maria Thoreau.

44. "Like summer friends, Flies of estate and sunshine"—George Herbert, *The Answer*.

45. Thoreau was obviously thinking of the many Biblical references (such as Heb. xii : 13) to a "straight path" through life.

46. Young Georgie Bartlett of Concord has said that he thought from the excitement stirred up over Thoreau's jailing he was seeing a Siberian exile or John Bunyan himself. (Walter Harding, *The Days of Henry Thoreau*, New York: Knopf, 1965, p. 205.)

47. Silvio Pellico (1789-1854), the Italian revolutionary, wrote an autobiography with this title that was popular in the 1840's.

48. *I.e.*, a Mohammedan.

49. Orpheus, son of the Muse Calliope, according to Greek mythology, played his lyre with such a masterly hand that rivers ceased to flow, beasts forgot their wildness, and even the mountains were moved to listen.

50. George Peele, *The Battle of Alcazar* (1588-89), II. ii. Thoreau has slightly reworded and modernized the text and, as John T. Onuska, Jr. has pointed out (*New York Times Book Review*, February 6, 1966, p. 47), has wrenched its meaning from its original context. These lines were not included in the *Aesthetic Papers* version.

51. Daniel Webster (1782-1852), famed Massachusetts senator.

52. *I.e.*, those who framed the American Constitution.

53. Speech on the Texas question, delivered by Webster on December 22, 1845. *Writings*, IX, 57.

54. Speech on the bill to exclude slavery from the territories, delivered by Webster on August 12, 1848. *Writings*, X, 38.

55. "Let your loins be girded about."—Luke xii : 35.

56. Confucius. This sentence was not included in the *Aesthetic Papers* version.

57. Note that this essay, like all of Thoreau's, ends on an essentially optimistic note.

PART IV

The Critical Overview

THE CRITICS LOOK AT
"CIVIL DISOBEDIENCE"

". . . There is about it ['Civil Disobedience'] the awful grandeur of a strong man who has made up his mind. Whether you approach it as art, idealism, anarchy or autobiography, it is not to be thrust aside. Like the granite conc of a mountain, solid and lonely, it fills the sky; you can avoid it only by keeping your eye on the ground. Thoreau could write in many veins; he could be fanciful, pithy, humorous, poetic or merely truculent. But this time he wrote unequivocally to be understood. 'What is once well done is done forever,' he declares. Although the essay sprang immediately from his hatred of slavery, and of a government that countenanced slavery, he did it so well that it is done forever and begins on its own merits as great literature and idealistic thinking."

> J. Brooks Atkinson, "Civil Disobedience,"
> *New York Times Book Review* (January 13, 1929).

"... Taken by itself ['Civil Disobedience'] alone, it is a somewhat astonishing performance. This Yankee transcendentalist quite evidently has turned philosophical anarchist. But read in the light of Emerson's *Journals,* or in the light of Godwin's *Political Justice,* it is easily comprehensible. It is no more than transcendental individualism translated into politics, with all comfortable compromises swept away. Its sources run straight back to eighteenth-century liberalism with its doctrine of the minimized state—a state that must lose its coercive sovereignty in the measure that the laws of society function freely. Very likely Thoreau had never read Godwin, yet his political philosophy was implicit in *Political Justice.* . . .

"... To neither thinker is there an abstract state, society or nation—only individuals; and to both, the fundamental law is the law of morality. Political expediency and the law of morality frequently clash, and in such event it is the duty of the individual citizen to follow the higher law. Thoreau went even further, and asserted the doctrine of individual compact, which in turn implied the doctrine of individual nullification; no government, he said, can have any 'pure right over my person or property but what I concede to it.'"

Vernon Louis Parrington, *Main Currents in American Thought* (New York: Harcourt, Brace, 1930), II, 409–410.

". . . His 'Civil Disobedience,' indeed, is little more than a sermon on that very doctrine [of the Declaration of Independence which justifies revolution when perversion of the forces of government has reached a point where revolt is more useful than forbearance], and his refusal to pay his taxes was his mode of putting it in practice."

James Mackaye, "Introduction," *Thoreau: Philosopher of Freedom* (New York: The Vanguard Press, 1930), p. xiii.

"As an admirer of Thoreau, I thought I detected similarities in Gandhi's ideas and Thoreau's philosophy. The first question I put to him was: 'Did you ever read an American named Henry D. Thoreau?' His eyes brightened and he chuckled.

"'Why, of course I read Thoreau. I read *Walden* first in Johannesburg in South Africa in 1906 and his ideas influenced me greatly. I adopted some of them and recommended the study of Thoreau to all my friends who were helping me in the cause of Indian independence. Why, I actually took the name of my movement from Thoreau's essay, "On the Duty of Civil Disobedience," written about eighty years ago. Until I read that essay I never found a suitable English translation for my Indian word, *Satyagraha*. You remember that Thoreau invented and practiced the idea of civil disobedience in Concord, Massachusetts, by refusing to pay his poll tax as a protest against the United States government. He went to jail, too. There is no doubt that Thoreau's ideas greatly influenced my movement in India.'

"I think I was perhaps the first to discover the curious fact that the wizened Hindu mystic adopted from the hermit philosopher of Concord the strange political concept of nonviolent civil disobedience which deeply influenced the teeming millions in India; that the example of the gentle visionary of Walden Pond inspired millions to defy without arms the power of the world's greatest empire; that the ideas of the sensitive man in Concord who detested violence and bloodshed had after eighty-one years resulted in hundreds of deaths, the injury of ten thousand, and imprisonment of perhaps a hundred thousand in India on the other side of the world."

Webb Miller, *I Found No Peace* (New York: Simon and Schuster, Inc., 1936), pp. 238–239.

"We cannot perceive what we canonize. The citizen secures himself against genius by ikon-worship. By the touch of Circe-Citizen's wand, the divine troublemakers are metamorphosed into porcine stone embroidery. . . .

"There is an uncanny shrewdness in those well-governmented Americans who have looked at Thoreau as a kind of cranky male sybil, a crabbed and catarrhal water-sprite of our woodland culture. Little wonder that his 'Civil Disobedience' lies dormant and half-forgotten as a curio in libertarian and anarchist anthologies. Imagine were it otherwise: what state would dare render sincere homage to its greatest male malefactor, Henry David Thoreau? What society of men so beautifully groomed in submission could countenance 'Civil Disobedience'. . . .

"The State is adept in the mysteries of evasion and interment. Henry David Thoreau is honored; but his books lie buried like the fresh barley seeds stored by Joseph in granaries and scattered in Pharaohs' tombs. Administrative Philistia needs no economic astrologer to help it read 'Civil Disobedience' or 'Walden.' Society is clairvoyant, knows how to govern, when to load its musket, when to erect an obelisk,—and when to canonize. The iconographer, the antiquarian, is the state's best servant and art's most formidable foe. Sequestrate the writer into an 'early American' of a Golden Age of Letters, and you refuse him. You disclaim him by a spurious exaltation of his period.

". . . No other American but Bourne has taken such a deep and accurate measure of the secular despotisms of government as Thoreau. None has had his ethics—a social conscience with a moral auditory nerve which responded to the finest shadings of injustice. Writing with the intense Christian fervour of a Leo Tolstoy, Thoreau says in 'Civil Disobedience,' 'Is there not a sort of blood shed when the conscience is wounded?'

"Thoreau was an opposer: he was against society, slaves, institutions, church and politics; and the sum of his giant negations is a more illuminating text for a way toward understanding the subtler courtesies and gentler urges of men than those weedy and unkempt affirmations in Whitman's 'Democratic Vistas.' The 'canting peal' of Sunday morning service was as raucous to his ethical sense organs as the sound of air-biting drayman's whips was to the ears of Schopenhauer. 'I am too high-born to be propertied,' he said. Announcing his total disallegiance to organized government, he wrote: 'Know all men by these presents, that I, Henry Thoreau, do not wish to be regarded as a member of any Incorporated Society which I have not joined.' To him the body politic was 'covered with scoriae and volcanic cinders, such as Milton imagined.' "

Edward Dahlberg, *Do These Bones Live*
(New York: Harcourt, Brace, 1941), pp. 8–10.

"Thoreau is . . . to be distinguished from the ranters against the State. He does not reject the State as an instrument. In fact he approves it as such. He notes that 'the progress from an Absolute to a Limited Monarchy, from a Limited Monarchy to a Democracy, is a progress toward a true respect for the individual.' But he would go beyond Democracy 'towards recognizing and organizing the rights of man.' The reader of our great Americans, Jefferson, Lincoln, and Whitman, finds them entirely in agreement. American Democracy is an instrument, not an end in itself. It is an instrument for 'recognizing and organizing the rights of men.' "

> Dr. Arthur E. Briggs, "Thoreau's Man In Society,"
> *Thoreau "The Cosmic Yankee"* (Los Angeles: Roman Forum & Rocker, 1946), p. 30.

"Thoreau's indictment of the state was obviously the hyperbole of the advocate. He did not approve of license. 'To speak practically and as a citizen, unlike those who call themselves no government men, I ask for, not at once no government, but at once a better government.' Although he believed that the ideal society needed no government—and in this he was the philosophical anarchist—he was too wise ever to expect perfection. In denouncing the state he aimed at assuring the individual the freedom to which he was entitled. And if his anarchist direction leads to a blind alley, his bold method of moral resistance is still pertinent."

> Charles A. Madison, *Critics & Crusaders*
> (New York: Holt, 1947), p. 192.

"Of all the spiritual representatives of American liberalism, Thoreau was perhaps the most profound and consistent. His so-called individualism was not the result of negative attitude toward society but of a natural relation of man to man. 'I love mankind,' he said, 'but I hate the institutions of the dead unkind. Man executes nothing so faithfully as the wills of the dead, to the last codicil and letter. They rule the world, and the living are but their executors.'"

> Rudolf Rocker (tr. Arthur E. Briggs),
> *Pioneers of American Freedom* (Los Angeles:
> Rocker, 1949), p. 31.

"Looked at as a political credo the essay is just wrong. In it Thoreau offends common sense and our common understanding of the need for organized society or government. The opening paragraphs exhibit this first error, his failure to recognize the primacy of the state. Most of us would admit Jefferson's dictum, 'That government is best which governs least,' if taken as a statement of policy in operation. But when Thoreau starts his essay with this famous remark, he leaves little doubt that he proposes the comment only in its extreme interpretation and so denies the fundamental principle that man needs the state, so needs it that he must as a rational being provide it for his own social welfare.

"But Thoreau looks on government at best as but an expedient, not as an essential need with real rights and powers no matter how small the minimum exercise of these might in practice be. Even the abuse of power by a standing government does not deny its claim to *some* power; even as a standing army, to follow Thoreau's figure, may have justification despite the wrongs it perpetrates. When government activity becomes an obstacle to business or commerce, it is to be judged by its seeking the common good and not measured by Thoreau's norm of its success in letting men alone."

C. Carroll Hollis, "Thoreau and the State,"
The Commonweal, L. (September 9, 1949), p. 531.

"It is quite clear that Thoreau's mind was totally closed to the democratic conception of politics as a never-ending process of compromise and adjustment. As a matter of fact, if the politics of 'action from principle,' with its insistence on ends, is shorn of metaphysics, it appears as little more than the old and familiar doctrine that the end justifies the means. Comparison of 'Civil Disobedience' and 'A Plea for Captain John Brown' underlines the fact that in Thoreau's mind both passive resistance and violent action were *right* if employed toward the accomplishment of ends whose truth is predicated on the complete assumption of responsibility by the individual for his acts.

"Just as nonviolent resistance as an instrument of politics is proper if the state interferes with an individual's principles, so violence can be justified. Given Thoreau's moral intransigence, it is not surprising to find that he would round out his basic position by eulogizing an event which only the most rabid Abolitionists supported as politically justifiable. John Brown, Thoreau came to believe, was not only right in holding that a man has 'a perfect right to interfere by force with the slaveholder, in order to rescue the slave'; but the doctrine that the end justifies the means was given explicit expression: 'I shall not be forward to think him mistaken in his method who quickest succeeds to liberate the slave.' The decisive question, Thoreau finally felt, was not 'about the weapon, but the spirit in which you use it.' And he would write in his *Journals*: 'I do not wish to kill nor to be killed, but I can foresee circumstances in which both these things would be by me unavoidable.'"

Heinz Eulau, "Wayside Challenger," *Antioch Review*, IX (Winter, 1950), pp. 519–520.

"In 1846, as the legend goes, the writer Henry David Thoreau was jailed in Concord, Mass., for refusing to pay his taxes as a political protest. Visiting Thoreau, Ralph Waldo Emerson peered through the cell bars, and asked: 'What are you doing in there?' Replied Thoreau: 'What are you doing out there?'

"Most of us are still 'out there,' but . . . American artists are being judged, convicted and fired solely on charges of professional informers. . . . American writers have been forced to choose jail rather than betrayal of their beliefs. . . . American scholars are losing their posts as a result of the imposition of loyalty oaths which have nothing to do with their competence as free and honest teachers. . . .

"All of these things are taking place because too many of us have been silent. Americans don't like thought control, or a climate which invites false denunciation by anyone about anyone. We don't like the denial of passports to American citizens on grounds of what they think, or the refusal of visas to foreigners because of their political convictions.

"Democracy could never have been built by men whose hands were shaking with fear. Democracy cannot be preserved, or wars won, by men whose hands shake with fear, or who fail to speak up against hysteria and injustice.

"What are we doing out here? This is not an advertisement calling on you to join anything or to contribute money. We only ask you to raise your voice for freedom. The voices of bigotry

77

and aggressive intimidation are loud and raucous throughout the country today. If the voices of decency and courage remain silent, the right of everyone to live and work in peace and freedom may be lost.

"Americans, like Thoreau in his Concord jail, have believed that this is a land where the right of free opinion is sacred. When Americans are jailed or lose their jobs because of their thoughts, a precious part of each of us is locked away.

"We ask you to protest violations of the right to free opinion. Those who control the great media of American communications should hear from Americans who cherish the right to determine for ourselves, free from hysterical denunciation and the fears of fanatics, what all of us can see, hear, read and learn.

"Speak up for freedom! It doesn't matter how—it may be done in a letter to your Congressman, to a radio network or sponsor, or to your school or college. It may be in conversation in your own home. But speak up!

Louis Adamic - Nelson Algren - Stringfellow Barr - Roger Butterfield - Gilbert Gabriel - Jack A. Goodman - A. B. Guthrie - Margaret Halsey - John Lardner - Alexander Meiklejohn - Arthur Miller - Harry Overstreet - Artur Schnabel - William Shirer - Louis Untermeyer - Mark Van Doren - Ira Wolfert"

> Louis Adamic, *et al., New York Times,*
> [paid advertisement], Jan. 15, 1951.

"An inordinate respect for the law, that is to say, for expedients, inevitably resulted, Thoreau believed, in the degeneration of the moral fiber of the individual. The process of degeneration was already far advanced. Soldiers, as a 'natural result of an undue respect for law' had surrendered their manhood and had so become 'mere shadow[s] and reminiscence[s] of humanity'; public servants of all kinds, in pledging their allegiance to the inferior standard of expediency represented by the government, had restricted the 'free exercise' of their 'moral sense' and had so 'put themselves on a level with wood and earth and stones.' Being a good citizen was a far cry from being a good man. The good citizen—the legislator, politician, lawyer or minister—rarely made any moral distinctions, but followed the expedient course prescribed for him by law; a very few '*men* serve[d] the State with their consciences also, and so necessarily resist[ed] it,' and consequently were 'commonly treated by it as enemies.' Thoreau's chief purpose in 'Civil Disobedience' was to wean men away from their adherence to an insidious relativism and to persuade them to return again to the superior standard of absolute truth."

Wendell Glick, "Civil Disobedience: Thoreau's Attack on Relativism," *Western Humanities Review*, VII (Winter '52 '53), p. 35.

"To appreciate Thoreau's negations we need only be willing to examine, as candidly as he examined, the real nature of those institutions and values that provoked his dissent. He abominated chattel slavery; he rebelled against the Mexican War; he poured his wrath on the executioners of John Brown; he decried the inhuman, debasing qualities of a cash-nexus society which reduced so many people to 'lives of quiet desperation.' Was this perversity? Let apologists for injustice think so. The perceptive reader of *Walden, Civil Disobedience, A Plea for Captain John Brown* discerns what is affirmative in these works and is thrilled by their passion for truth, their sensitivity to wrong, their bold and incorruptible humanism."

> Samuel Sillen, "Thoreau in Our Time" in *Looking Forward* (New York: International Publishers, 1954), p. 154.

"Only those who are otherwise willing to obey the law . . . could have a right to practice civil disobedience against unjust laws. It was quite different from the behavior of outlaws, for it was to be practiced openly and after ample notice. It was not likely, therefore, to foster a habit of lawbreaking or to create an atmosphere of anarchy. And it was to be resorted to only when all other peaceful means, such as petitions and negotiations and arbitration, had failed to redress the wrong."

> Krishnalal Shridharani, as quoted in Robert B. Downs, *Books that Changed the World*, (New York: New American Library of World Literature, 1956), p. 79.

"A prophet does not mince words or juggle theories, nor did Thoreau. Everything he did, he did from high principle and without compromise. In all of his fulminations against society, law, government, and his fellow men, there are remarkably few second thoughts or hesitations, and, I think, no admission that he was ever wrong on any fundamental point of opinion or conduct. This provokes uneasiness at the start about half of what he says, for unshakable self-assurance about anything and everything is not calculated to instil faith—rather the reverse, in those who are not blind followers of the master. The truth is that Thoreau is not merely often wrong, but wrong to an incredible degree, to a degree that makes his mind appear very lopsided. That is the penalty he pays for pledging his allegiance to inspiration rather than to ratiocination and factual evidence. . . .

"Naturally Thoreau does not like majority rule. To replace it he offers, typically, the mystery of individual inspiration. . . .

"There is no more insidious political theory than this. When consciences conflict—and antagonism is never worse than when it involves two men each of whom is convinced that he speaks for goodness and rectitude—what then? Who is to decide? Who except the Leader with a capital *L?* Thoreau's theory has overtones of Rousseau's Legislator who can do what he pleases with the people under his control because he alone can fathom the holy intentions of the General Will. It points forward to Lenin, the 'genius theoretician' whose right it is to force a suitable class consciousness on those who do not have it, and to the horrors that resulted from Hitler's 'intuition' of what was best for Germany.

81

"Nevertheless, Thoreau had one saving grace—he was not so dominated by an obsession as to let it cloud over everything else in his mind. It may have been simply the working of his self-centeredness, but at least he never brooded long enough to be driven finally to plunge frantically into the melee. If he talked grotesquely when the seizure was on him, these were spells that came and went, and in between, as he implies, he was able to ignore them. Hatred of slavery compels John Brown to pick up his rifle and head for Kansas. Thoreau curses and raves in print —and then strolls into the woods to look, with completely engrossed attention, for the first breaking up of the ice on the pond, for the earliest buds of spring, for the appearance of beaver and blacksnake after their winter's hibernation."

Vincent Buranelli, "The Case Against Thoreau,"
Ethics, LXVII, (July, 1957), pp. 262, 265, 266, 267.

". . . in a Democracy a man's supreme loyalty is not to the Government but to the integrity of his own mind, to the promptings of his conscience, to his God. In putting his loyalty to these values first, Democracy dares to affirm that a man will in the long run serve his country and his government best. . . .

"The task of preserving and extending this genuine loyalty among us is a very difficult one. It requires great faith, great trust, great patience, and great courage. It also requires common sense. The only way to keep the liberties of America alive is to keep them alive; to encourage, not punish, Americans for thinking and speaking freely. The only way to save democracy is to be democratic and prove that democracy works. The only way to win the kind of loyalty we want and desperately need is to climb out of this pit of stale conformity and to challenge men once more to think bold new thoughts about themselves, their country, and their world. Our spiritual heritage is great because men and women in the past dared to do this without fear. The spiritual challenge in the present is to us, the living, to go on doing it. It is only so that we can win the right to be called loyal to the heritage of our past and the unrealized hopes of our future."

Harry C. Meserve, "What is Loyalty?" First Unitarian Church, San Francisco, California. Undated mimeographed pamphlet [c. 1960].

". . . The very notion of 'civil disobedience,' for example, is now unthinkable. (Except in India, perhaps, where in his campaign of passive resistance Gandhi used this speech as a textbook.) In our country a man who dared to imitate Thoreau's behavior with regard to any crucial issue of the day would undoubtedly be sent to prison for life. Moreover, there would be none to defend him—as Thoreau once defended the name and reputation of John Brown. As always happens with bold, original utterances, these essays have now become classic. Which means that, though they still have the power to mold character, they no longer influence the men who govern our destiny. They are prescribed reading for students and a perpetual source of inspiration to the thinker and the rebel, but as for the reading public in general they carry no weight, no message any longer. The image of Thoreau has been fixed for the public by educators and 'men of taste': it is that of a hermit, a crank, a nature faker. It is the caricature which has been preserved, as is usually the case with our eminent men."

Henry Miller, *Stand Still Like the Hummingbird*
(Norfolk, Conn.: James Laughlin, 1962), p. 112.

"According to . . . Thoreau . . . the most liberal government becomes a tyranny when it denies the right of the individual to be responsible for his intellectual and moral integrity. It can overrule him, yes, but he must somehow resist.

"Political philosophers would be quick to point out the inherent weakness of the argument. If the individual is to determine his own rights, what authority is left to distinguish between enlightened resistance to the rule of a State and anarchy which will inevitably dissolve the State itself?

"Thoreau has not attempted to resolve this problem or give a direct answer. The essay as a whole does, however, suggest that he would have answered that you must have faith in man, you must believe that an intuition to what is necessary for survival is a reality in human nature. And that is the only possible answer."

Anonymous, "Mahatma Gandhi and Thoreau,"
India News (October 1, 1962), p. 8.

"Thoreau's essay on civil disobedience marked a significant transition in the development of non-violent action. Before Thoreau, civil disobedience was largely practised by individuals and groups who desired simply to remain true to their beliefs in an evil world. There was little or no thought given to civil disobedience for producing social and political change. Sixty years later, with Gandhi, civil disobedience became, in addition to this, a means of mass action for political ends. Reluctantly, and unrecognised at the time, Thoreau helped make the transition between these two approaches. . . .

"The term 'civil disobedience' does not appear in the text of Thoreau's essay itself. In English the term had dual connotations. 'Civil' means civil behavior, i.e., polite, gentle, humane, non-violent. This meaning was emphasised by Gandhi. 'Civil' also means that which pertains to a community of citizens, or pertains to or befits a citizen, as in Thoreau's original title: *Resistance to Civil Government*. This dual meaning expresses two essential aspects of civil disobedience. It is peaceful, and it is the response of a member of a political society to its demands and activities. . . .

"The reasons for civil disobedience vary. It may be practised reluctantly by those who have no desire to disturb the *status quo*, but wish only to remain true to their convictions. Or, it may be undertaken with the limited aim of changing a particular policy or regulation which is regarded as unjust. It may also be used, along with other forms of non-violent action, in times of major social or political upheaval as a substitute for violent revolution with the aim of undermining, paralysing and disintegrating a regime which is regarded as inherently unjust and oppressive."

Gene Sharp, "Introduction," *Thoreau On the Duty of Civil Disobedience*, Peace News Pamphlets (January, 1963), pp. 1, 3, 4.

"The justification for civil disobedience is that *it is obedience to a higher law than the one transgressed.* 'I march to a different drummer,' said Thoreau in his American classic, *Walden.* It is plain that to disobey the law openly, formally and nonviolently can be a moral act of the highest kind, for it is an offering of oneself, one's freedom, in protest against an unjust enactment. This is quite a different thing from furtive disobedience to the law, as in violation of traffic regulations, cheating on one's income tax, or as in the ill-starred Prohibition era, when millions of Americans indulged in wholesale evasion of an imprudent law."

> Rory McCormick, "When Laws Should Be Broken,"
> *Ave Maria,* (Nov. 30, 1963), p. 12.

"The message of Thoreau is . . . valuable . . . for it serves as a constant reminder that it shall not profit a man to possess the world if he loses his own soul—that there is an unrelenting conflict between the Transcendentalist and the 'Organization man' and that no matter how impressive the external trappings one covers oneself with, what is invaluable in the last resort is the individual."

> Braj Kumar Nehru, "Henry David Thoreau: A Tribute,"
> in *The Thoreau Centennial,* ed. Walter Harding (Albany: State University of New York, 1964), p. 119.

"Thoreau recognized with extraordinary prescience the nature of the weaknesses which immobilize a nation in the presence of a mortal crisis. It was in relation to slavery that Thoreau felt his fellow citizens were losing their souls. One weakness was that they permitted money to come between them and the objects of their duty—not simply money, but the things which money could buy. And thus, he said, as did Jesus before him, men gain the whole world but lose their souls. He saw the opponents of reform in Massachusetts to be 'not a hundred thousand politicians at the South, but a hundred thousand merchants and farmers here, who are more interested in commerce and agriculture than they are in humanity, and are not prepared to do justice to the slave and to Mexico, cost what it may.' The rich man is sold to the institution that makes him rich."

William Stuart Nelson, "Thoreau and the Current Non-Violent Struggle for Integration," *Concord Journal,* an address delivered on July 11, 1964.

"Most unfortunately [today] non-violence is often giving way to violence which loses the moral force and persuasion so essential to Thoreau, Gandhi, and King. Civil disobedience must also consist in direct non-compliance with what is essentially an unjust law, so that there is clearly established an open, honest protest that has some direct relationship with injustice. Opening water faucets to deplete a water supply, clogging highways to the World's Fair, or booing the President who was at the moment championing a new Civil Rights law is simply another form of injustice, insensitivity, or inhumanity—alienating friends and confirming enemies. Looting, inane destruction of property, hooliganism and violence, personal injury, and irresponsibility are as far from the moral foundations espoused by the true promoters of civil rights as injustice is far from justice, order from disorder, humanity from inhumanity. . . ."

The Reverend Theodore M. Hesburgh, address given before the meeting of the American Academy of Arts and Sciences, Boston, Mass., November 11, 1964.

". . . [Thoreau] saw that because civil disobedience passed beyond speech-making or picketing or boycotting or other peaceful methods of protest, and actually broke the law, it would necessarily involve serious personal risks. Here lay Thoreau's greatest contribution to the methodology of social protest. On the basis of his own limited experience with civil disobedience, he was able to reach the conclusion that recent experiences in Mississippi have only too well confirmed: the man who would practice civil disobedience must be totally committed because he risks jail or even death whenever he makes the decision to disobey society on a matter of principle. Civil disobedience, unless it arises from sheer lust for martyrdom, must be the outward, visible expression of an inward, complete dedication.

"It was this aspect that appealed so strongly to Gandhi. He saw that mob violence or revolutionary war aroused hatred on both sides; whereas, civil disobedience and similar nonviolent techniques of social reform demanded self-discipline and commitment from their practitioners. By being moral techniques themselves, they were more apt to break down hostilities and evoke moral responses from the society they were directed against. Martin Luther King, Jr.'s recent reaffirmation of nonviolence in the Negro civil rights movement can be seen as yet another refusal to depart from the proposition inherent in Thoreau's civil disobedience, namely, that the means of attaining a moral goal cannot be divorced from that goal itself."

Bruce Watson, "The Origin of Civil Disobedience," *Fellowship*, XXXI (March, 1965), pp. 15–16.

". . . Thoreau was the first political theorist to advocate a selective and agitatory disobedience directed toward a government he had no intention of supplanting with a new regime. . . . He had a contempt for the political process in and of itself, a contempt reflected in his refusal ever to vote. . . . Voting is compromise; it shows some willingness to live by standards reached in cooperation with others, and he recognized no norms outside himself."

> Garry Wills, "Why did Thoreau start it?"
> *National Catholic Reporter*, November 17, 1965.

"Thoreau's 'Civil Disobedience' stood for me, and for my first leader in the resistance movement, as a shining light with which we could examine the policy of complete passivity which our government had ordered for the whole Danish population. The German Wehrmacht behaved well if not provoked, but the Gestapo was boundlessly cruel. Non-violence, as a means of resistance, was completely unfit for this scum of the worst gangsters of Germany from whom they were all recruited. I lent Thoreau's books to friends, told them about him, and our circle grew. Railroads, bridges, and factories that worked for the Germans were blown up."

> Anonymous, "Thoreau and the Danish Resistance,"
> in *Thoreau in Our Season* (ed. John H. Hicks),
> (Univ. of Mass. Press, 1966), p. 20.

This timely reissuance of Henry David Thoreau's principles of civil disobedience is accompanied by an informative and graceful introduction. The now-famous incident of Thoreau's arrest for nonpayment of taxes is recounted, as is the history of the publication of *Civil Disobedience*. Most important is the story of the world-wide influence exerted by Thoreau's words. The introduction traces this influence in Gandhi's movement to free India in the 1940s, in the Danish resistance against the Nazis, and in civil disobedience movements in the United States. Thoreau's ideas have been forcefully implemented by the abolitionists, conscientious objectors, and civil rights leaders, among others. Also mentioned is past governmental opposition to the publication and dissemination of *Civil Disobedience*.

A unique section, "The Critics Look at 'Civil Disobedience,'" scans criticism and commentary on the essay since it was first published in Elizabeth Peabody's *Aesthetic Papers* to the present.

Variorum Civil Disobedience is fully annotated and stands as a companion volume to the *Variorum Walden*, also edited by Walter Harding (Twayne, 1965).